Book 1
Cryptography
By Solis Tech

&

Book 2
Malware
By Solis Tech

Book 1
Cryptography
By Solis Tech

Cryptography Theory & Practice Made Easy!

Cryptography: Cryptography Theory & Practice Made Easy!

Table of Contents

Introduction

I want to thank you and congratulate you for purchasing the book, *Cryptography*.

This book contains tips and techniques on how to build cryptosystems – even if you're just a complete beginner.

This eBook will help you learn about the history and basic principles of cryptography. It will teach you the different aspects of message encryption. In addition, you will learn how to establish cryptosystems. Aside from discussing modern/digital encryption schemes, this book will teach you how to use different types of "practical" ciphers.

Thanks again for purchasing this book. I hope you enjoy it!

Chapter 1: Cryptography – History and Basic Concepts

The Origin of Cryptography

During the ancient times, people needed to do two things: (1) to share information and (2) protect the information they are sharing. These things forced individuals to "encode" their messages. This "encoding" process protects the message in a way that only the intended recipient can understand the information. That means the data will remain secure even if unauthorized parties get access to it.

The art and science of protecting information is now known as "cryptography." The term "cryptography" was formed by fusing two Greek terms, "Krypto" (which means "hidden") and "graphene" (which means writing).

According to historians, cryptography and "normal" writing were born at the same time. As human civilizations progressed, people organized themselves into groups, clans, and kingdoms. These organizations led to the creation of concepts such as wars, powers, sovereignty, and politics. Obviously, these ideas involve information that cannot be shared with ordinary citizens. The group leaders needed to send and receive information through protected means. Thus, cryptography continued to evolve.

The Contributions of Egyptians and Romans

1. Egyptians

The oldest sample of cryptography can be found in Egypt. Ancient Egyptians used hieroglyphs (i.e. a system of writing that involves symbols and images) to share and record pieces of information. In general, these symbols and images are only intelligible to the priests who transmitted messages on behalf of the pharaohs. Here is a sample hieroglyph:

Fig. 1 - Egyptian Hieroglyphs

Several thousands of years later (around 600 to 500 BC), Egyptian scholars started to use simple substitution codes. This style of encoding involved the replacement and/or combination of two or more alphabets using a secret rule. This rule was considered as the "key" in retrieving the real message from the coded "garbage."

2. <u>Romans</u>

Ancient Romans used a system of cryptography known as the Caesar (or Shift) Cipher. This system depends on moving each letter of the message by a certain number (three is the most popular choice). To decode the information, the recipient simply needs to "move" the letters back using the same number. Here is an example:

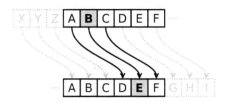

Fig. 2 – Caesar Cipher

Cryptography – Fundamental Concepts

Encryption – This is the process of converting information into an unintelligible form. It helps in securing the privacy of the message while it is being sent to the recipient.

Decryption – This process is the exact opposite of encryption. Here, the encoded message is returned to its natural form.

Important Note: Encryption and decryption requires specific rules in converting the data involved. These rules are known as the key. Sometimes, a single key is used to encrypt and decrypt information. However, there are certain scenarios where these two processes require different sets of keys.

Plaintext and Ciphertext – The term plaintext refers to data that can be read and used without the application of special techniques. Ciphertext, on the other hand, refers to data that cannot be read easily: the recipient needs to use certain decryption processes to get the "real" message.

7

Authentication – This is probably one of the most important aspects of cryptography. Basically, authentication serves as a proof that the information was sent by the party claimed in the encoded message.]

Let's illustrate this concept using a simple example: John sent a message to Jane. However, before replying, Jane wants to make sure that the message really came from John. This verification procedure can be conducted easily if John does "something" on the message that Jane knows only John can do (e.g. writing his signature, including a secret phrase, folding the letter in a certain way, etc.). Obviously, successful decryption of the message will be useless if the information came from an unwanted source.

Integrity – Loss of integrity is one of the biggest problems faced by people who use cryptography. Basically, loss of integrity occurs whenever the message gets altered while it is being sent to the receiver. Unnecessary and/or unwanted modifications in a message may cause misunderstanding and other issues. Because of this, the message must be protected while it is being delivered. Modern cryptographers accomplish this through the use of a cryptographic hash (i.e. a hash function that is extremely difficult to invert, modify, or recreate).

Non-Repudiation – This concept focuses on ensuring that the sender cannot deny that he/she sent the encoded message. In the example given above, it is important to make sure that John cannot deny the fact that he was the one who sent the message. Modern cryptography prevents this "sender repudiation" using digital signatures.

Chapter 2: The Modern Cryptography

For some people, modern cryptography is the foundation of technology and communications security. This type of cryptography is based on mathematical concepts like the number theory, the probability theory, and the computational-complexity theory. To help you understand modern cryptography, here is a comparison of the "classical" and "modern" types of cryptography.

Classical Cryptography

1. It utilizes common characters (e.g. letters and numbers) directly.

2. It relies heavily on the "obscure is secure" principle. The encryption and decryption processes were considered as confidential information. Only the people involved in the communication can access such data.

3. It needs an entire cryptosystem (will be explained in the next chapter) to complete the "confidential" transfer of information.

Modern Cryptography

1. It relies on modern technology like binary data sequences.

2. The information is encoded through the use of mathematical algorithms accessible to the public. Here, security is achieved through a "secret key" which is used as the foundation for the algorithms. Two factors ensure that "outsiders" cannot access the information even if they have the correct algorithm:

   a. It is extremely difficult to compute such algorithms. Thus, it is hard to extract any information from them.

   b. The absence or presence of secret keys.

3. The encryption doesn't involve the entire cryptosystem. Only the interested parties are required to participate in encoding and decoding the message.

Chapter 3: Cryptosystem – The Basics

A cryptosystem is the application of cryptographic methods and their appropriate coding environment (also called "infrastructure"). This system is used to add security to technology and communications services. Some people refer to cryptosystems as "cipher systems."

To illustrate the concept of cryptosystems, let's consider the following example:

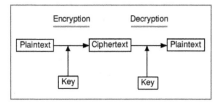

Fig. 3 – A Cryptosystem

In this example, the sender encrypts his message (i.e. the plaintext) through the use of a key. This process converts the plaintext into ciphertext. Once the receiver gets the ciphertext, he uses the same key to decrypt the information. Thus, the ciphertext will be turned into plaintext again.

As you can see, only the parties who have the "key" can access the shared information. Cryptosystems can be divided into these basic components:

- Plaintext – The information that needs to be shared and protected.

- Encryption Algorithm – The mathematical process that uses a plaintext and an encryption key to produce a ciphertext.

- Ciphertext – The coded version of the information. In general, cryptography protects the message itself, not the transmission. That means the coded message is sent through public channels such as emails. Thus, anyone who can access the selected delivery channel can intercept or compromise the message.

- Decryption Algorithm – It is a mathematical process that creates plaintext from any given set of ciphertext and decryption key. Basically, it reverses the encryption process done earlier in the transmission of the message.

- Encryption Key – The value provided by the sender. In creating the ciphertext, the sender enters this key (along with the plaintext) into the encryption algorithm.

- Decryption Key – The value known by the recipient. The decryption key is always related to the encryption key used for the message. However, these keys don't have to be identical. The recipient enters the decryption key and the ciphertext into the decryption algorithm in order to get the plaintext. The collection of all decryption keys for a cryptosystem is known as a "key space."

There are times when an interceptor (also called "attacker") tries to get the encoded message. In general, interceptors are unauthorized entities who want to access the ciphertext and determine the information it contains.

The Two Kinds of Cryptosystems

Currently, cryptosystems are divided into two kinds: (1) Symmetric Key Encryption and (2) Asymmetric Key Encryption. This way of classifying cryptosystems is based on the method of encryption/decryption used for the entire system.

The major difference between the symmetric and asymmetric encryptions is the connection between the encryption and decryption keys. Generally speaking, all cryptosystems involve keys that are closely related. It is impossible to create a decryption key that is totally unrelated to the code's encryption key. Let's discuss each kind of cryptosystems in more detail:

Symmetric Key Encryption

Cryptosystems that belong to this kind have a single key. This key is used to encrypt and decrypt the information being sent. The study of symmetric encryption and systems is known as "symmetric cryptography." Some people refer to symmetric cryptosystems as "secret key" systems. The most popular methods of symmetric key encryption are: IDEA, BLOWFISH, DES (Digital Encryption Standard), and 3DES (Triple-DES).

During the 1960s, 100% of the cryptosystems utilized symmetric encryption. This method of encrypting and decrypting information is so reliable and efficient that it is still being used even today. Businesses that specialize on Communications and Information Technology consider symmetric encryption as the best option available. Since this kind of encryption has distinct advantages over the asymmetric one, it will still be used in the future.

Here are the main characteristics of symmetrically encrypted cryptosystems:

11

- Before transmitting the message, the sender and the receiver must determine the key that will be used.

- The key must be changed regularly to avoid any intrusion into the cryptosystem.

- A stable form of data transmission must be established to facilitate easy sharing of the key between the involved parties. Since the keys must be changed on a regular basis, this mechanism may prove to be expensive and complicated.

- In an organization composed of "x" individuals, to facilitate two-way communication between any two members, the required number of keys for the entire system is derived using the formula: "x * (x-1)/2."

- The keys used are often small (i.e. measured through the number of bits involved), so the encryption and decryption processes are faster and simpler compared to those used for asymmetric systems.

- These cryptosystems do not require high processing capabilities from computer systems. Since the keys used are small and simple, ordinary computers can be used to establish and manage the cryptosystem.

Here are the two problems usually encountered when using this kind of cryptosystem:

- Key Determination – Before any message can be transmitted, the sender and the receiver must determine a specific symmetric key. That means a secure and consistent way of creating keys must be established.

- Trust Issues – Because all the people involved use the same key, symmetric key cryptography requires the sender to trust the receiver, and vice versa. For instance, if one of them shares the key with an unauthorized party, the security of the entire cryptosystem will be ruined.

Modern day communicators say that these two concerns are extremely challenging. Nowadays, people are required to exchange valuable data with non-trusted and non-familiar parties (e.g. seller and buyer relationships). Because of these problems, cryptographers had to develop a new encryption scheme: the asymmetric key encryption.

Asymmetric Key Encryption

These cryptosystems use different keys for encrypting and decrypting the message. Although the keys involved are dissimilar, they still have a logical and/or mathematical relationship. It is impossible to extract the message using a decryption key that is totally unrelated to the encryption key.

According to cryptographers, this mode of encryption was developed during the 20th century. It was developed in order to overcome the challenges related to symmetric key cryptosystems. The main characteristics of this encryption scheme are:

- Each member of the cryptosystem should have two different keys – a public key and a private key. When one of these keys is used for encryption, the other one must be used for decryption.

- The private key is considered as confidential information. Each member must protect the private key at all times. The public key, on the other hand, can be shared with anyone. Thus, public keys can be placed in a public repository. As such, some people refer to this scheme as "public key encryption."

- Although the private and public keys are mathematically related, it is practically impossible to determine a key using its "partner."

- When Member1 wants to send information to Member2, he needs to do three things:

    o Obtain Member2's public key from the public repository.

    o Encrypt the message.

    o Transmit the message to Member2. Member2 will acquire the original message using his private key.

- This mode of encryption involves larger and longer keys. That means its encryption and decryption processes are slower compared to those of symmetric encryption.

- The asymmetric key encryption requires high processing power from the computers used in the cryptosystem.

Symmetric key encryption is easy to comprehend. The asymmetric one, however, is quite difficult to understand.

You may be wondering as to how the encryption and decryption keys become related and yet prevent intruders from acquiring a key using its "partner." The answer to this question lies in mathematical principles. Today, cryptographers can create encryption keys based on these principles. Actually, the concept of asymmetric key cryptography is new: system intruders are not yet familiar with how this encryption works.

Here is the main problem associated with asymmetric key cryptosystems:

- Each member needs to trust the cryptosystem. He/she has to believe that the public key used for the transmission is the correct one. That person must convince himself that the keys in the public repository are safe from system intruders.

  To secure the cryptosystem, companies often use a PKI (Public Key Infrastructure) that involves a reputable third party organization. This "outside organization" manages and proves the authenticity of the keys used in the system. The third party company has to protect the public keys and provide the correct ones to authorized cryptosystem members.

Because of the pros and cons of both encryption methods, business organizations combine them to create safer and practical security systems. Most of these businesses are in the communications and information technology industries.

Kerckhoff's Principle

During the 19th century, a Dutch cryptographer named Auguste Kerckhoff identified the requirements of a reliable cryptosystem. He stated that a cryptosystem must be secure even if everything related to it – except the keys – are available to the public. In addition, Mr. Kerckhoff established six principles in designing new cryptosystems. These principles are:

1. The cryptosystem needs to be unbreakable (i.e. in a practical sense). This excludes the system's vulnerability to mathematical intrusions.

2. The system should be secure enough that members can still use it even during an attack from unauthorized entities. The cryptosystem needs to allow authorized members to do what they need to do.

3. The keys used in the system must be easy to change, memorize, and communicate.

4. The resulting ciphertexts must be transmissible by unsecure channels such as telegraph.

5. The documents and devices used in the encryption system must be portable and easy to operate.

6. Lastly, the system must be user-friendly. It should not require high IQ or advanced memorization skills.

Modern cryptographers refer to the second rule as the Kerckhoff principle. They apply it in almost all encryption algorithms (e.g. AES, DES, etc.). Experts in this field consider these algorithms to be completely secure. In addition, these experts believe that the security of the transmitted message relies exclusively on the protection given to the private encryption keys used.

Maintaining the confidentiality of the encryption and decryption algorithms may prove to be a difficult problem. Actually, you can only keep these algorithms secret if you will share them with a few individuals.

Today, cryptography must meet the needs of internet users. Since more and more people gain access to hacking information and advanced computers, keeping an algorithm secret is extremely difficult. That means you should always use the principles given by Kerckhoff in designing your own cryptosystems.

Chapter 4: Different Types of Attacks on Cryptosystems

Nowadays, almost every aspect of human life is affected by information. Thus, it is necessary to safeguard important data from the intrusions of unauthorized parties. These intrusions (also called attacks) are usually classified based on the things done by the intruder. Currently, attacks are classified into two types: passive attacks and active attacks.

Passive Attacks

Passive attacks are designed to establish unauthorized access to certain pieces of information. For instance, activities such as data interception and tapping on a communication channel are considered as passive attacks.

These activities are inherently passive: they do not attempt to modify the message or destroy the channel of communication. They simply want to "steal" (i.e. see) the information being transmitted. Compared to stealing physical items, stealing data allows the legitimate owner (i.e. the receiver) to possess the information after the attack. It is important to note that passive data attacks are more harmful than stealing of physical items, since data theft may be unnoticed by the receiver.

Active Attacks

Active attacks are meant to alter or eliminate the information being sent. Here are some examples:

- Unauthorized modification of the message.

- Triggering unauthorized transmission of data.

- Modification of the data used for authentication purposes (e.g. timestamp, sender's information, etc.).

- Unauthorized removal of information.

- Preventing authorized people from accessing the information. This is known as "denial of service."

Modern cryptography arms people with the tools and methods for preventing the attacks explained above.

The Assumptions of a Cryptosystem Attacker

This section of the book will discuss two important things about system attacks: (1) cryptosystem environments and (2) the attacks used by unauthorized parties to infiltrate cryptosystems.

The Cryptosystem Environment

Before discussing the types of data attacks, it is important to understand the environment of cryptosystems. The intruder's knowledge and assumptions about this factor greatly influence his choices of possible attacks.

In the field of cryptography, three assumptions are made about the attacker and the cryptosystem itself. These assumptions are:

1. Information about the Encryption Method – Cryptosystem developers base their projects on two kinds of algorithms:

    i.   Public Algorithms – These algorithms share information with the public.

    ii. Proprietary Algorithms – These algorithms keep the details of the cryptosystem within the organization. Only the users and designers can access information about the algorithm.

    When using a proprietary (or private) algorithm, cryptographers obtain security through obscurity. In general, these are developed by people within the organization and are not thoroughly checked for weaknesses. Thus, private algorithms may have loopholes that intruders can exploit.

    In addition, private algorithms limit the number of people that can join the system. You can't use them for modern communication. You should also remember Kerckoff's principle: "The encryption and decryption keys hold the security of the entire cryptosystem. The algorithms involved can be shared with the public."

    Thus, the first assumption is: "The attacker knows the encryption and decryption algorithms."

2. Obtainability of the Ciphertext – The ciphertext (i.e. the encrypted information) is transmitted through unsecured public channels. Because of this the second assumption is: "The attacker can access ciphertexts created by the cryptosystem."

3. Obtainability of the Ciphertext and the Plaintext – This assumption is more obscure than the previous one. In some situations, the attacker may obtain both the plaintext and the ciphertext. Here are some sample scenarios:

i.   The attacker convinces the sender to encrypt certain pieces of information and gets the resulting ciphertext.

ii. The recipient may share the decrypted information with the attacker. The attacker obtains the corresponding ciphertext from the communication channel used.

iii. The attacker may create pairs of plaintexts and ciphertexts using the encryption key. Since the encryption key is in the public domain, potential attackers can access it easily. It's a "hit and miss" type of tactic.

Cryptographic Attacks

Obviously, every attacker wants to break into the cryptosystem and obtain the plaintext. To fulfill this objective, the attacker simply needs to identify the decryption key. Obtaining the algorithms is easy since the information is available publicly.

This means the attacker focuses on obtaining the secret decryption key. Once he/she gets this information, the cryptosystem is broken (or compromised).

Cryptographic attacks are divided into several categories. These are:

- BFA (Brute Force Attack) – Here, the intruder tries to find the decryption key by entering all possible information. For instance, the key contains 8 bits. That means the total number of possible keys is 256 (i.e. 2^8). The attacker tries all of these keys in order to obtain the plaintext. The longer the key, the longer the time needed for successful decryption.

- COA (Ciphertext Only Attack) – This tactic requires the complete set of ciphertexts used for a message. When COA gets the plaintext from the given ciphertexts, the tactic is considered successful. Attackers may also get the corresponding encryption key using this attack.

- CPA (Chosen Plaintext Attack) – This attack requires the attacker to work on the plaintext he/she selected for encryption. Simply put, the attacker has the plaintext-ciphertext combination. It means the task of decrypting the information is easy and simple. It is the first part of the attack – convincing the sender to encrypt certain pieces of information – that presents the most difficulties.

- KPA (Known Plaintext Attack) – With this tactic, the attacker should know some parts of the plaintext. He/she has to use this knowledge to obtain the rest of the message.

- Birthday Attack – This is a subtype of the brute force approach. Attackers use this tactic when working against cryptographic hash functions. Once the intruder finds two inputs that produce similar values, a collision is said to occur: the hash function is broken and the system is breached.

- MIM Attack (Man in the Middle Attack) – This attack is particularly designed for public key cryptosystems. In general, these systems require the exchange of keys before the actual transmission of the ciphertext. Here is an example:

  o Member1 wants to send a message to Member2. To do this, he sends a request for Member2's public key.

  o An intruder blocks the request and sends his own public key.

  o Thus, the unauthorized party acquires the information that will be sent by Member1.

  o To avoid detection, the intruder encrypts the data again and sends it to Member2.

  o The intruder uses his own public key. That means Member2 will see the attacker's key instead of Member1's.

- SCA (Side Channel Attack) – This attack is used to exploit the weaknesses of a cryptosystem's physical implementation. Here, the attackers ignore the system's algorithms and digital protection.

- Fault Analysis Attacks – When using this attack, the intruder looks for errors produced by the system. He/she uses the resulting information to breach the system's defenses.

- Timing Attacks – Here, attackers use the fact that different calculations require different processing times. These people can acquire some data about the message processed by a computer system. They do this by measuring the time used by the computer in performing its calculations.

- Power Analysis Attacks – These attacks are similar to the previous one. However, instead of time, they use the amount of power consumed by the computer system. This information is used to determine the nature of the plaintext.

An Important Note About Cryptographic Attacks

The attacks explained above are theoretical and highly academic. Actually, most of those attacks are defined by cryptography instructors. Some of the attacks you read about involve unrealistic assumptions about the attacker and/or the system's environment.

However, these attacks have excellent potential. Attackers may find ways to improve them. It would be great if you will still consider these attacks when designing your own cryptosystems.

Chapter 5: Traditional Cryptography

You have learned about the basics of modern cryptography. You also discovered the different tools that you can use in designing your own cryptosystems. One of the powerful tools at your disposal is the symmetric key encryption: a mode of encryption that uses a single key for the entire communication process.

This chapter will discuss this mode further so you will know how to apply it in developing cryptosystems.

Old Cryptographic Systems

At this point, you have to study the cryptosystems used in the ancient times. These "old systems" share similar characteristics, which are:

- These cryptosystems are based on the symmetric mode of encryption.

- The message is protected using a single tool: confidentiality.

- These systems use alphabets to facilitate encryption. In contrast, modern cryptosystems use digital data and binary numbers to encrypt a message.

These old systems are called "ciphers." Basically, a cipher is just a group of procedures performed in order to encrypt and decrypt data. You may think of these procedures as the "algorithms" of these ancient cryptosystems.

1. The Caesar Cipher

This cipher is based on a single alphabet. Here, you can create a ciphertext just by replacing every letter of the message with a different one. Cryptologists consider this cipher as the simplest scheme today.

The Caesar Cipher is also called "shift cipher," since each letter is shifted by a fixed number. If you are using the English alphabet, you can use the numbers from 0 to 25. The people involved must choose a certain "shift number" before encoding the plaintext. The number will serve as the encryption and decryption key for the entire communication process.

How to Use the Shift Cipher

1. The sender and the receiver select a shift number.

2. The sender writes down the alphabet twice (i.e. a-z followed by a-z).

3. That person gets the plaintext and finds the appropriate letters. However, he moves the letters based on the shift number selected. For example, if

they are using the number 1, he will replace the letter "A"s with "B"s, the "B"s with "C"s, and so on.

4. The encryption procedure is done once all of the letters have been shifted.

5. The sender transmits the ciphertext to the receiver.

6. The receiver moves the letters of the ciphertext backwards, depending on the shift number being used.

7. Once all of the letters have been shifted, the decryption process is completed. The receiver can use the information he received from the sender.

The Cipher's Security Value

This is not a secure system since the possible encryption keys are extremely limited. If you are using the English alphabet, your possible keys are restricted to 25. This number is not enough for those who need more security. In this situation, an attacker may acquire your key just by carrying out a thorough key search.

2. The Simple Substitution Cipher

This is an improved version of the Caesar Cipher. Instead of using numbers to determine the ciphertext, you will choose your own equivalent for each letter of the alphabet. For instance, "A.C... X.Z" and "Z.X... C.A" are two simple permutations of the letters in the English alphabet.

Since this alphabet has 26 letters, the total permutations can be derived through this formula: $4\text{x}10^{26}$. The people involved can select any of these permutations to create the ciphertext. The permutation scheme serves as the key for this cryptosystem.

How to Use this Cipher

1. Write down the letters from A to Z.

2. The involved parties choose a permutation for each letter. For example, they might replace the "A"s with "F"s, the "B" with "W", etc. These new letters don't need to have any logical or mathematical relationship with the letter they represent.

3. The sender encrypts the plaintext using the selected permutations.

4. The message is sent to the receiver.

5. The receiver decodes the ciphertext using the chosen permutations.

The Cipher's Security Value

This cipher is way much stronger than the Caesar Cipher. Even strong computer systems cannot decode the ciphertext since the possible permutations (i.e. 4×10^{26}) are too many. Cryptosystems based on this cipher can stop attackers that rely on a brute force approach. However, this substitution system is based on a simple scheme. In fact, attackers have succeeded in breaking letter permutations in the past.

The Monoalphabetic and Polyalphabetic Ciphers

Monoalphabetic Ciphers are ciphers that rely on a single encryption system. In other words, a single encryption alphabet is used for each "normal" alphabet throughout the entire communication process. For instance, if "C" is encoded as "X", "C" must be written as "X" each time it appears in the plaintext.

The two encryption systems discussed above belong to this type.

Polyalphabetic Ciphers, on the other hand, involve multiple encryption alphabets. The encryption alphabets may be switched at different segments of the encryption procedure. Here are two examples of polyalphabetic ciphers:

The Playfair Cipher

This encryption scheme uses pairs of letters to create encryption alphabets. Here, the people involved must create a table where letters are written down. The table used is a 5x5 square (i.e. 25 in total): the squares inside the table hold the letters of the alphabet. Since there are 26 letters in the English alphabet, a letter must be omitted. Cryptographers often omit the letter "J" when using this cipher.

The sender and the receiver must choose a certain keyword, say "lessons." They must write this keyword in the key table, from left to right. In addition, they should not repeat letters. Once the word is written down, the sender/receiver must complete the table using the unused letters (i.e. alphabetically arranged). With the word "lessons" as the keyword and J omitted, the key table should look like this:

L	E	S	O	N
A	B	C	D	F
G	H	I	K	M
P	Q	R	T	U
V	W	X	Y	Z

How to Use this Cipher

1. You should split the message into diagraphs (i.e. pairs of letters). If the total number of letters is an odd number, you should add a Z to the last letter. As an example, let's encrypt the word "human" using the key table created above. It will look like this:

   HU MA NZ

2. Here are the encryption rules:

   a. If both letters are in the same column, you should use the letter under each one. You have to go back to the top if you are using the bottom letter. In our example, N and Z are in the same column. Thus, this pair becomes FN.

   b. If both letters are placed in the same row, use the letter located at the right of each one. You need to go back to the first letter of the row if you are working on the rightmost letter. (This rule doesn't apply to our example.)

   c. If none of the previous rules apply, create a rectangle using the pair of letters. Afterward, use the letters on the opposite corner of the correct letters. Work on the letters horizontally. According to this rule, the HU pair is converted to MQ (look at the key table). MA, on the other hand, becomes GF.

3. Using these rules, the word "human" becomes MQ GF FN when encrypted using the Playfair Cipher.

4. You just have to reverse the process if you want to decrypt the message.

Cryptography: Cryptography Theory & Practice Made Easy!

The Playfair Cipher's Security Value

This scheme is stronger than the systems discussed earlier. Attackers will have a difficult time analyzing all of the possible keys. In general, cryptologists use this cipher to protect important information. Lots of people rely on the Playfair Cipher since it is easy to use and doesn't require special tools.

The Vigenere Cipher

This encryption scheme uses a word (also known as text string) as the key. This key is used to change the plaintext. For instance, let's use the word "human" as the key. You should convert each letter into its numeric value (i.e. A = 1, B = 2, etc.). In our example:

$$H = 8, U = 21, M = 13, A = 1, N = 14$$

How to Use this Cipher

1. If you want to encrypt "cold water," you have to write the letters down. Then, write the key numbers (i.e. 8, 21, 13, 1, and 14) under the words, one number for each letter. Repeat the numbers as necessary. It looks like this:

C	O	L	D	W	A	T	E	R
8	21	`13	1	14	8	21	13	1

2. Shift the letters of the normal alphabet according to the number written on the table. Here it is:

C	O	L	D	W	A	T	E	R
8	21	13	1	14	8	21	13	1
K	J	Y	E	K	I	O	R	S

3. As you can see, each letter of the plaintext is moved by a different amount – the amount is specified by the key. The letters of your key should be less than or equal to that of your message.

4. To decrypt the message, you just have to use the same key and shift the letters backward.

The Vigenere Cipher's Security Value

This cipher offers excellent security: better than the three ciphers discussed above. Cryptographers use this encryption system to protect military and political data. Because of its apparent invulnerability, security experts call this the "unbreakable cipher."

Chapter 6: Modern Cryptography Schemes

Nowadays, cryptographers use digital data to establish encryption systems. This data is often represented as sets of binary digits (also called "bits"). Modern cryptosystems must process these binary strings to create more strings. Symmetric encryption techniques are categorized based on the procedures performed on the digital information. These categories are:

Block Ciphers

These ciphers group the digital data into separate blocks and process them one at a time. The number of bits contained in a data block is predetermined and unchangeable. Two popular block ciphers, AES and DES, have block sizes of 128 and 64, respectively.

In general, a block cipher uses a set of plaintext data and produces a set of ciphertext data, usually of the same size. Once the block size is assigned, it can no longer be modified. The block size used for the system doesn't affect the strength of encryption techniques involved. The strength of this cipher relies on the length of its key.

Block Size

Although you can use any block size, there are some things you have to consider when working on this aspect of your cryptosystem. These are:

- Avoid small block sizes – Let's assume that a block size is equal to m. Here, the total number of possible plaintext combinations is 2^m. If an intruder acquires the plaintext data used for previous messages, he/she can initiate a "dictionary attack" against your cryptosystem. Dictionary attacks are performed by creating a dictionary of ciphertext and plaintext pairs generated using an encryption key. You should remember this simple rule: the smaller the block size, the weaker the system is against dictionary attacks.

- Don't use extremely large block sizes – Large block sizes mean more processing time for your computer system. Cryptographers working on large bit sizes experience efficiency issues. Often, the plaintext must be padded in order to get the desired block size.

- Use a block size that is a multiple of 8 – Computers can easily handle binary digits that are multiples of 8. You can take advantage of this fact by choosing a block size that has this mathematical property.

Different Types of Block Cipher Schemes

Cryptographers use a variety of block cipher encryption schemes in their systems. Here are some of the most popular block ciphers being used today:

- AES (Advanced Encryption Standard) – This cipher is based on Rijndael, an award-winning encryption algorithm.

- IDEA – This is considered as one of the strongest ciphers available. Its block size is equal to 64 while its key size is equal to 128 bits. Many applications utilize this encryption. For instance, the old versions of PGP (Pretty Good Privacy) protocol used IDEA extensively. Because of patent issues, the utilization of this encryption scheme is restricted.

- DES (Digital Encryption Standard) – This is the most popular block cipher during the 1990s. Because of their small size, DES ciphers are now considered as "broken ciphers."

Stream Ciphers

With this scheme, the information is encrypted one binary digit at a time. The resulting ciphertext is equivalent to the data processed (e.g. 10 bits of plaintext produce 10 bits of ciphertext). Basically, stream ciphers are block ciphers with a block size limit of 1 bit.

Chapter 7: The Pros and Cons of Cryptography

This chapter will discuss the pros and cons of using cryptography.

The Pros

Today, security experts consider cryptography as one of their most useful tools. It provides four things needed for modern communication:

1. Authentication – Cryptographic techniques like digital signatures prevent spoofing and data forgeries.

2. Confidentiality – Encryption schemes protect information from unauthorized parties.

3. Non-repudiation – The digital signatures used in cryptography prove the identity of the sender. Thus, disputes regarding this factor are prevented.

4. Data Integrity – Cryptography involves hash functions that can maintain the integrity of the data being transmitted.

The Cons

Nothing is perfect. Here are the problems associated with cryptography:

- Legitimate users may encounter issues when accessing well-encrypted information. This can turn into a disaster if a certain piece of information has to be obtained quickly.

- Constant availability of information – a basic aspect of communications and information technology – is hard to secure when using cryptography.

- Cryptosystems prevent selective access control. Some organizations need to provide exclusive file access to certain officers. When using cryptosystems, these organizations will have problems in giving selective access to their chosen members. This is because cryptosystems apply the same security measures on every file.

Conclusion

Thank you again for purchasing this book!

I hope this book was able to help you master the basics of cryptography.

The next step is to build your personal cryptosystems so you can easily encrypt messages.

Finally, if you enjoyed this book, please take the time to share your thoughts and post a review on Amazon. It'd be greatly appreciated!

Thank you and good luck!

Book 2
Malware
By Solis Tech

Malware Detection & Threats Made Easy!

Malware: Malware Detection & Threats Made Easy!

Table of Contents

Introduction

I want to thank you and congratulate you for purchasing the book, *"Malware: Malware Detection & Threats Made Easy!"*.

This book contains proven steps and strategies on how to avoid, detect and remove malware.

Malware creators are very creative, employing both technical and social means to spread malware. Simply installing antivirus software is no longer enough. This book explains how malware spreads in order to arm the reader with information on how to manage its threat.

Thanks again for purchasing this book, I hope you enjoy it!

Chapter 1 – Malware

Computers are inherently dumb. They can accept and input data, can process it at high-speed, and can return the results almost instantly. However, users need to tell the computer what to do in the form of codes. We call these codes programs, applications, scripts or software, but they are essentially the same. They give instructions to the computer. What the computer does will depend on the instructions given to it. Tell it to do something useful and it will. Give it instructions to perform a malicious task and it will do it without question. Even computers with artificial intelligence are simply following instructions that simulate human's way of thinking.

Computers do not care who gives the instructions. As long as the instructions are loaded into memory, the computer will process it accordingly. Upon startup, a short set of instructions will tell the computer to load and launch the operating system or OS. The OS in turn executes startup instructions that it finds. These include preparing the input and output drivers, as well as launching other background tasks. Having done that, the OS awaits command from its user to execute other applications.

Malware developers take advantage of these key concepts. They find vulnerabilities in the operating and network system that will allow them to install malware and have it running in the background. Vulnerabilities are bugs in the program that can let malware writers load additional code and execute it. These bugs or programming errors do not always appear during the testing stage.

Some malware writers use social engineering to trick victims into installing malware into their computers. They use the computer's connection to internal and external networks to propagate the malware. They infect shared storage to spread malware among colleagues. They hack into servers to install malicious code that will infect site visitors. They can do this because computers will run any executable code that is loaded into its memory.

What is Malware?

Malware is short for malicious software. It is a general term for a code that compromises a computer and instructs it to do malicious tasks, often without the knowledge or permission from the computer's owner. Early malware refers to programming challenges and pranks like programs that delete user files, but recent malware refers to targeting servers to make them inaccessible or for financial gains.

Home computers are not safe, either. Cybercriminals are using home computers to launch attacks on servers in addition to stealing personal information to access online bank accounts. Some advertisers adopt malware, too. They no longer wait for users to visit their sites, but install malware into a victim's computer so they can modify browser settings and change the default home page, eventually advertising their products every time a user opens the browser. They sometimes change the default search engine, replacing it with engines that track user habits to benefit advertisers.

Mobile devices are not safe, either. Today's mobile devices are computers with features and capabilities that are comparable to older computers. Mobile devices, like smartphones and tablets, are vulnerable because they require applications to work. If users inadvertently download a compromised application, then there is a possibility that malware can compromise their mobile devices, too.

A future malware playground is Internet of Things. It is a term for consumer devices like smart home appliances and vehicles loaded with small computers to provide intelligent functionality. These intelligent appliances connect to the Internet for remote control and administration. Having computers on these things, it may not be long until we can see malware on these devices too.

Remember that appliance manufacturers are not IT companies; hence, they may not have the capability to implement data security in their products. A hacker compromising a manufacturer's server could trigger a firmware update on connected appliances and make it perform additional functions, including attacking other servers on the Internet. It may sound like an event from a science-fiction movie, but this reality is possible.

What is the Difference Between a Malware and a Virus?

Many people confuse malware with viruses. A virus is a type of malware, while malware include viruses and other malicious software.

The first malware were viruses, and developers wrote antivirus software to eliminate these malicious programs. Even when viruses evolved to other forms, people still call them viruses and antivirus companies are using the same term even if they are targeting other malware variants.

Viruses are no longer common on their original form. With antivirus vendors constantly updating their algorithms, malware developers have to come up with new variants to avoid detection, often employing social engineering to propagate malware faster by tricking victims to install it along with legitimate software.

If we look at how malware developers remain active over the years, we can surmise that it is a financially rewarding business; therefore, we can expect cybercriminals to continue developing better malware while antivirus companies play catch-up. The only way to combat malware is to understand the threat it presents, how it spreads and propagates, how to detect it, and how to remove.

What are Potentially Unwanted Programs (PUPs)?

People love free software; however, developers need to earn money too. Malware developers see this as an opportunity to spread malware while providing revenue to free-software developers. What they come up with are installers for legitimate software that also install malware during installation. Antivirus companies call these Potentially Unwanted Programs instead of malware since victims give explicit permission to install them. They have no way of knowing if users allow the installation on purpose or unknowingly installs them.

Why would Users Give Permission to Install PUPs?

Most users do not bother reading user agreements that installers display during installation. Instead, they simply click on the default buttons or press enter. Even if users will read the agreements and prompts, some may not understand the message and assume that they are installing software that is necessary for the main program to work. Unfortunately, PUPs are easy to install, but are often frustrating to remove from the system. Most have more than one instance running such that removing a copy will trigger the second copy to re-install it. Many recent PUPs affect users' browsers, which can be very annoying.

How to Detect the Presence of Malware?

Users familiar with their computer will sometimes notice unusual behavior. Some are obvious, like the browser's looks suddenly changing. Other users may lose their files or the file types are changed. Users may even see system errors that were not present before.

Some changes are not visual, like a program accessing the hard disk and making noise even when the computer is idle. Malware accessing an external server can slow down Internet connection. Infected computers can also be unresponsive when hidden processes are running and using up the computer's memory.

Before assuming that malware may be causing the problem, try restarting the computer and leave it for a few minutes without running any program. If the computer is still slow, then there may be an unwanted background program running, but it still needs confirmation.

On Windows, check the hard disk space by opening any folder and clicking Computer on the left. A hard disk with very little space can slow down the computer and malware may not be the cause.

If there is plenty of hard disk space available, run the Task Manager by holding Ctrl+Alt+Del and selecting it from the menu. Click on the Performance tab and observe the real-time graph. Both the CPU and memory usage should be relatively flat if the computer is idle. An active graph could mean that a hidden program is busy. Click the Applications tab to confirm. There should be no application listed if the user did not execute a program. If there is no program listed and the CPU or memory graph is active then there could be a malware running in the background.

To see the process that is using up the memory, click on the Process tab, then click Memory to display the list in descending order. Check its Image name and description. Right-click on a name, then select Properties to get more details. Use a search engine to validate suspicious names.

The Networking tab can also give clues on the presence of malware. There should be no network activity if the computer is idle. If the network is slow and this graph is active, then a hidden program is accessing an external server or computer.

These are just some ways of detecting the possible presence of malware. Without knowing what the malware exactly is; however, it could be difficult to remove it manually.

Most leading antivirus software can detect and remove malware. For home users, there are free versions available that offer basic protection with the option to purchase upgrades for additional features.

A Note on USB flash drives

With the popularity of USB flash drives, spreading malware via USB is easier. Malware can automatically execute when the user opens a USB flash drive. Once in computer memory, inserting another USB drive will infect it. To prevent this, do not view the contents of a USB flash drive after it mounts. Instead, right-click on the drive's name or icon, then select the scan option from the antivirus. This will remove malware in the flash drive before using it.

If there are signs that a USB drive is infected, but the antivirus does not detect it, install another antivirus program. Some antivirus solutions are not good at detecting USB-based malware.

Antivirus solutions can prevent the installation of malware to some extent. However, there are malware that can still get through if the user is not aware of how they propagate. The best way to prevent malware from infecting computers is to understand how each type works.

The succeeding chapters give an insight into the various forms of malware. It also provides information on how they spread so that users can avoid infecting their computers. Prevention is still the best cure against malware. However, avoiding malware is not easy.

Chapter 2 – Virus

Viruses are the earliest forms of malware and they date back to the time before personal computers became popular. A virus is simply a program that can replicate itself on the same computer. Even without malicious intent, creating many copies of a virus code can quickly fill up the memory and slow the computer down. However, an unmodified virus cannot spread to other computers by itself even if the computers are on a network. Getting the virus inside a computer is the challenge for virus creators.

To avoid detection, virus creators modify legitimate programs by inserting malicious codes. When these programs launch, the virus loads into memory and scans the computer for other executable codes to infect. The virus code stays active in memory until the computer shuts down and the cycle starts again if the user runs the infected program.

Boot Sector Virus

Some viruses attack the boot sector of the computer's bootable disks. The boot sector is an area of a disk that a disk drive initially reads and loads into memory. It contains the startup code that will load other components of the operating system. When the boot sector is infected, the virus loads into memory every time the computer starts, ensuring that it is active without waiting for the user to run an infected program. Since the disk operating system can fit in diskettes in the early days of personal computers, starting a clean computer with an infected bootable diskette can also spread the virus to that computer.

Be Careful when Using Shared Resources

Viruses can spread through sharing. When a user mounts a removable storage media on an infected computer while a virus is active, the virus attempts to infect programs that it finds on the mounted media as well. In the early days, this applies to floppy diskettes and external hard drives, but infections are more common today on flash USB drives.

Once the user connects an infected storage to another computer and runs an infected program, the virus activates and infects the other programs in the new computer as well. This makes users who mount USB drives on shared computers at risk if the computer has no sufficient antivirus protection installed. For this reason, avoid connecting USB drives at Internet cafes and on other public computers.

Even shared documents can carry viruses. Some productivity software allows scripts or macros to automate common tasks. Scripts and macros are small, but powerful programs; hence, they can spread viruses, too. Executing an infected macro will also compromise other documents on the same computer. Worse, sending a copy of an infected document can also infect the receiver's computer.

Are Early Viruses Malicious?

Some early viruses started as programming challenges. There was a game that was named Core Wars where the objective is to create a program that loads in memory, then replicate and terminate other programs running on the same memory space. The competing programs create copies of the code while overwriting enemy codes to terminate them. The program that remains in control is the winner.

Other early versions are simply annoying. Two programmers wrote the Brain virus because users were illegally copying their diskettes. The Brain virus simply displays information about the programmers. The Brain virus spread to computers in other countries.

Computers were not widely connected before and the worst thing that a virus can do is to delete files or make them inaccessible. This is exactly what early destructive viruses did. Some programmers wrote viruses that display something interesting while deleting computer files.

Birth of Antivirus Companies

It was not long before other programmers started writing codes to remove viruses, turning the process into a never-ending game of cat and mouse. Virus creators are continually discovering new computer vulnerabilities that they can take advantage of, while antivirus developers update their codes to combat new virus strains. It has become a never ending battle between malware developers and antivirus companies.

Antivirus programs initially identify specific viruses using their signatures. Signatures are like patterns or fingerprints that identify specific viruses. Virus creators responded by continually creating virus variants that require new methods of detection to keep up. This is why antivirus programs update their databases almost daily.

Antivirus can only play catch up if they rely solely on signatures. Modern antivirus programs detect possible viruses by their behavior in addition to signatures.

Most free antivirus software in the market can eliminate common virus threats so not having one installed is not an excuse. While they retain the name, current antivirus software can detect and remove other forms of malware. To enable additional protection, users can purchase additional features.

However, those who do not have a budget for paid features can still protect themselves from malware. The key is to understand how other forms of malware spread. The next chapters will explain these.

Chapter 3 - Worms

While viruses were a threat due to their ability to replicate, it is not a tool for mass infection because it cannot spread to other computers. The capability to spread over the network by itself is a feature of worms. Networks include local area networks (LAN) that are commonly found in offices, Wide Area Network (WAN) for remote offices, as well as worldwide networks like the Internet.

Early worm research had good intentions and started as helpful ideas. One worm crawls networked computers at night to run processor-intensive tasks, but saves the work and stays idle during the day so people can use the computers normally. It is a good idea that maximizes computer resources, similar to how modern cloud computing works. However, a programming error caused the computers to crash and they had to write another program to remove it.

Another programmer wrote a seemingly harmless worm to check the size of the Internet. The worm creates copies on target computers as it moved from one computer to the next. Due to a programming decision, it can install a copy even if it already exists on the same computer. Multiple running copies of the same worm can slow down the computer until it eventually crashes. A single worm was able to crash a big part the Internet.

Worms spread across the network by exploiting operating system and application vulnerabilities and taking advantage of insufficient data security practices. Nowadays, worms can also spread through social engineering. Social engineering is a technique used by hackers to trick users into unknowingly breaking standard data security precautions. Hackers can bypass a highly secure environment using social engineering.

Operating systems, or OS, are programs that manage computers and network equipment. Just like any program, it can have unintentional bugs and updating usually fixes the problem. Worms take advantage of these vulnerabilities to compromise the system.

If the OS or application developer releases an update before someone announces the vulnerability, then users have time to update the operating system before a malware exploits the vulnerability. This is why users should install updates especially if the patch is to address data security issues. Allowing automatic updates usually takes care of this, although there is a risk of automatically installing buggy updates.

On the other hand, if a malware creator releases a worm before the developer discovers the bug and releases an update, what we have is zero-day vulnerability. Modern antivirus companies address this by developing algorithms that detect malicious behavior. However, very aggressive antivirus solutions may lead to false positives.

False positives result when a scan reports the presence of malicious code when there is none. A good antivirus has few false positives. Third party evaluations can determine effective antivirus solutions with fewer false positives.

Mass-mailer worms

Worms can access email clients on user computers and use it to email copies of the worm to contacts in the address book. Some of these emails can trick recipients into downloading and installing the attachment, compromising the receiver's computer in the process. When this happens, that computer also becomes a mass-mailing tool. Unfortunately, these worms can also get a name from the address book and change the From field with this name. This means that the sender in the email may not be the email source, making the source difficult to track.

Aside from possibly compromising recipients' computers, mass mailers can also slow down network performance. If a worm infects several computers on the same network, then it could eat up all the allocated bandwidth. Worse, data security companies may include the computer's IP address in the blacklist for spamming. This can affect all computers in the network that shares the same public IP.

This is because most offices and home networks use a single public IP address for their router while individual computers get private IP addresses. Worse, some DSL subscribers may get a banned public IP address when their router restarts.

Always be wary of unsolicited emails with attachment even if it comes from a trusted source. A possible indicator of spam mail is when the receiver's name is not mentioned in the salutation. Bad grammar is also a sign of possible spam email.

Do not assume that the antivirus can catch all worm variants. Some worms change the file extension of the attached file. Users may think that they are opening an image file when in reality they are executing a worm. Worms do this by adding a .jpg to the filename, like picture.jpg.exe. Since many users configure their computers to hide the file extension, they do not see that the real extension is .exe because the filename they see is picture.jpg.

Some mass-mailer worms simply send spam advertisements. While they may not do damage to a user's computer, they can still trick victims into purchasing illegitimate products. These emails often have a web beacon, a small image that is loaded from an external server. Displaying this image will send the user's email address to the server, thereby validating that it is an active email account. It will then be a target for future spam emails.

Note that spammers do not use their own computers to send mass emails. They use email worms to prevent authorities from easily tracking them.

Worms for Phishing

Mass-mailer worms provide a great platform for quickly distributing malware. Malware creators use these worms to transport different payloads depending on their intention. One application of mass-mailers is for phishing.

Phishing is a form of identity fraud and is usually for stealing personal information for financial gains. It works this way.

Malware creators will copy a legitimate website's looks, specifically the login and profile pages. Websites of financial institutions like banks and payment platforms are examples of these. Next, they will create an email that looks like an official document coming from the target institutions. These emails often have a sense of urgency, requiring the user to log in to the website immediately to validate or change the password for security purposes. It will also include a link to the appropriate page for the user's convenience.

There lies the trick. Instead of linking to the legitimate page, it will redirect the user to the fake login page after clicking the email link. The URL will have the legitimate website's domain name, but with added characters. Some users may mistakenly believe that they are in the genuine site and proceed to log in. After entering the login detail, the next page may even require them to enter their credit card details for validation.

In reality, users can enter anything in the login page and it will be successful. The login page will simply save the credentials entered by the user, then display a page to get other credentials. When in doubt, users can initially enter incorrect login credentials to check if the site can really validate their account. If it accepts a wrong username or password, then there is no validation and the site is a fake.

Another way to verify if a website is a fake is through browsing all the menus and internal links before entering the login details. Malware creators may not go through the trouble of recreating an entire website's content.

To guard against phishing, never click on an email link to log in or change account details. Always type the known URL on the browser address bar. If clicking an email link asks the user to log in, then do not continue. Instead, type the correct URL in the browser's address bar before logging in.

The next chapter discusses other payloads that worms usually bring.

Chapter 4 - Trojan Horse

Trojans are malware that disguise as useful programs or install together with a legitimate application. Its name comes from the Trojan War, a part of Greek mythology where a wooden gift horse had soldiers inside that attacked the enemies while they were asleep to win the war. Similarly, a Trojan pretends to be a useful application, waiting for the user to launch it to execute the malicious code. Once activated, trojans will run in the background to do their designated task.

Trojans do not replicate and spread by themselves. They often combine with worms to infect other computers. Trojans are also common on unsolicited email attachments, while some users download them along with valid applications.

There are several types of trojans according to function.

Root kits

Root kit is not inherently bad. It is originally a tool for system administrators. It becomes bad if the creator installs it on a computer without permission from the owner, especially if the purpose is to do malicious tasks.

Some trojans will modify the computer's system for hackers to gain access. Root kits are tools for administrators that hide in the operating system while providing a back door for their creator. With privileged access, a root kit's owner can do almost anything to the infected computer remotely. Root kits are good at hiding their existence, making them difficult to detect. They can also delete any traces of malware installation. Root kits usually remain hidden until activated.

Bots

Bots are programs that perform automated tasks. Some bots, called spambots, flood websites with spam advertisements to generate traffic for another website. This is common in online forums and is the main reason why websites validate users before accepting their registration details. Some registration forms require the user to type the characters shown on an image to validate that the applicant is human. However, some spammers go around this by hiring humans to solve the test, although it comes at a cost.

A more malicious bot is one that employs brute-force attack on target websites. Most website owners do not build websites from scratch, but simply use an open source Content Management System (CMS) as a starting point. A CMS is a fully functioning website that allows the user to update content without writing a single line of HTML code. There are many templates to choose from, and websites owners can customize further by using their own graphic images. Using CMS, owners can update website content in a few clicks.

Many CMS software have the default username "admin" and some website owners do not bother changing it. Given the default administrator name, hackers only need to guess the password to take over the website and install malicious software. If it is a popular forum, then there is a risk that hackers can steal the member database.

To attack a website, hackers write bots that log into the target website and try to log in with passwords taken from a table of common passwords as well as words from the dictionary. A website that does not limit failed logins in a given period is a good target. Using a network of zombie computers, hackers are able to brute-force attack a website using bots with minimal risk of authorities tracking the attack's mastermind.

Stolen password databases from forums are not safe, either. Using rainbow tables, hackers can use brute-force to find the matching password for a member account. Since many users employ the same username and password on all sites they register to, this allows the hackers to hack into members' accounts on other sites as well.

Remote-controlled Bots

Malware developers can turn an infected computer into a remote-controlled bot that will perform malicious tasks, including attacking another computer. This is how they get away with Distributed Denial of Service attacks. Attackers do not use their own computers to flood a server, but instead, they use a large network of zombie computers from unsuspecting users. This also saves the attacker from bandwidth costs since the computer owner is paying for it. It also makes it difficult to track the attacker after it spreads from one computer to another.

One analysis of an affected computer shows that bots log into a chat server, waiting for commands from its master. Think of an army of sleeper bots just waiting patiently for a command to attack. Developers will typically just let an installed Trojan do nothing until they have an army of remote-controlled bots to launch a large-scale cyber-attack. The attacker then issues the command to attack from the chat server where the bots log in each time the infected computer is running.

Without good anti-malware software, the presence of a remote-controlled bot in a computer is difficult to detect since it sleeps until a command is given.

Keylogger

Some trojans can capture keystrokes as well as mouse movements in the background without the user knowing it. Called keyloggers, these programs can serve as surveillance software for a good purpose. Some parents use it to monitor children's online activity.

Trojan keyloggers can steal passwords and other personal credentials from unsuspecting users. It can wait for specific events, like users opening a login page, before starting to record user actions and keystrokes. It then sends the log to a remote server for its master.

Spyware

Spyware is another Trojan that collects sensitive information similar to a keylogger. However, it is not limited to monitoring key strokes to steal user credentials, but can also gather information about the user's online activity as well.

Adware

Adware is similar to spyware, but simply records and sends users' online activity and behavior as marketing data to marketers so they can display an appropriate advertisement. Some versions will redirect browser searches to advertisements while others will replace the default search engine with an advertiser's search engine.

Adware creators write these malware for revenue generation. Adware that alters browser settings is very difficult to remove. Antivirus software can remove adware from the computer, but usually leaves the modified browser settings. Saving browser bookmarks and restoring to factory settings can sometimes fix the problem.

Ransomware

Ransomware does what its name suggests. After installing the malicious code, it will either prevent access to the infected computer or encrypt the contents of its hard disk. Users will see a message demanding payment to disable the malware. The criminals behind typically employ money transfer services that are difficult to track. Add this to the fact that these cybercriminals usually live in other countries, making it difficult to run after them.

To spread ransomware, cybercriminals typically take over a legitimate website, usually without the owner's knowledge, to install the malware. They can also spread ransomware using drive-by downloads on the compromised website.

Drive-by Download

A drive-by download will allow the installation of malware by simply browsing an infected website. The user does not even have to click a download link. The affected website contains codes that check for browser or operating system vulnerabilities that allow for automatic download. The malware will install a program with a task to connect to another server to download the rest of the malware. The victim may not notice the download due to the initial programs' small size.

Some anti-malware software can warn if a website has malware when a user tries to access it.

Suspicious Packers

In order to avoid detection, suspicious packers compress and encrypt malware code. Good anti-malware utilities are aware of this and are able to detect the behavior of suspicious packers and prevent them from executing.

Removing Trojans

Most antivirus companies have software that can automatically remove trojans. While it is possible to remove Trojans manually, this may be a challenge since many have multiple copies running that can reinstall copies if the user deletes one.

When looking for good antivirus software, try the demo versions first. If satisfied, users can pay for other features that provide complete protection to the computer. Some of these protections include email and web surfing security.

In some cases, antivirus software can remove malware from the system, but not from the browser. If removing browser add-ons and restoring to factory setting does not work, uninstall the browser and download again.

Avoiding Installer Trojans

Among the popular sources of Trojans are free software installers. Software development costs money, and offering it free is not good for business. However, many people would prefer free over paid versions, especially when performing simple or one-time tasks. To address this, developers break down their programs by specific features, then allow third party marketers to offer them as free downloads in return for revenue to the developer. For example, one utility can convert AVI formats to MP4, while another can convert MP4 to MPG.

How can marketers earn money from offering free downloads? They get revenue by offering their services to advertisers. These marketers create installers for legitimate software, then include the option to install software from other companies. There is nothing wrong with that right, except that many users do not bother reading what they are installing. Unfortunately, many of these optional programs are adware that antivirus software tag as Potential Unwanted Programs (PUP).

An installer for free software will first confirm that users want to install the desired legitimate program. After the user clicks on the Continue or Next button, the installer will get the user's consent to install additional software along with a few descriptions of its benefits. Sometimes, the installer will display an End User License Agreement (EULA), something that no one ever reads, but simply agrees to. It is common to see more than one program added in the installation. The problem, however, is that the default buttons will install these extra programs if the user is not careful.

How can users avoid these additional installations, especially if the user is unsure if the other software is required? Most installers have a Decline button for optional installations. When an installer shows the Decline button, then that additional software is probably a PUP. Pay attention to the presence of Decline buttons.

Some installers have no separate dialog boxes for additional software installation. Instead, easy and custom install options are available, with the easy install as the default. What the user may not see is that the easy install option will sometimes install additional software. Click the custom install option when it is available and deselect unfamiliar applications.

Some antivirus may give an alert that the installer has a Trojan. Always scan the installer after downloading. Users can do this by selecting the installer, right clicking then selecting the Scan option to run the antivirus. This is also a good practice after inserting USB devices.

Users can perform additional verification after each installation. In Windows, simply select Programs and Features from the control panel, then click the Installed On tab. Sort the list in descending order. The programs with the current date are the ones included in the installation. Select suspicious programs and click uninstall. To verify applications, enter the program name in a search engine to see what it does.

Chapter 5 – Threats on Mobile Devices

Mobile technology is now a part of people's everyday lives. Smartphones today are very powerful. They are no longer just for voice and text, but for accessing the Internet and playing games as well. Though not as efficient as personal computers, users can perform most tasks on their smartphones.

For those who require laptop capability at more portable form factor, tablets are a blessing. Those who want the small size of a phone, but with a bigger screen like a tablet, can choose a phablet. Mobile computing is now a reality.

As computers, these mobile devices can be targets of malware. To minimize these, Android and IOS, the leading mobile platforms, have screening policies in place to reduce the chances of malware getting into the official stores. Additionally, updates to the operating system often include security fixes for known vulnerabilities to strengthen the security of devices. Installing the latest updates, when available to the user's mobile device, addresses possible malware problems.

By default, users can only download apps from the official stores. This is Google Play for Android and App Store for IOS. However, a checkbox on Android's setting will allow the user to download from any external server. There lies the problem.

The price for mobile apps is quite low compared to their PC counterparts. However, many users still do not wish to pay for the apps they download, despite their low prices. Malware creators take advantage of this by making commercial apps available for free download on third party servers. By simply deselecting a default Android setting, users can now download a paid app for free.

Unfortunately, for them, these modified apps may contain malware written for mobile devices. Once installed on a mobile device and executed, these malware take over the device and do what PC malware often do. Some malware may steal user credentials while others may display unwanted advertisements. These malware can make the devices very slow, rendering them unusable. Restoring to factory settings may be the only option for some.

IOS has no checkbox to allow downloading of apps from unofficial sites, but bugs in the operating systems can allow jailbreaks. Jailbreaks are IOS hacks that allow users to customize their devices. It also allows users to install unofficial apps. Some of these apps may have malware and can compromise the device.

Malware creators are smart and can always find ways around a secure system. One company created a Windows application that allows users to download apps for free then transfer them to their IOS device. This comes with a risk, however, since some of these apps may also have malware.

Malware creators started targeting IOS developers in China. They did this by making local copies of Apple's development platform since downloading from Apple's official servers is quite slow for developers located in China. Unfortunately, the unofficial installer has malware that infects the apps they are developing. Some of these apps made their way into the App Store before they were discovered and removed.

Another malware creator took advantage of enterprise certificates. These certificates are used by companies to install their own apps on IOS devices without approval from Apple. Malware creators are tricking users to install an enterprise certificate so they can install apps with malware on victims' devices. Many users who do not understand the implications are at risk.

Apple quickly released an update to IOS that prevents this malware from installing. Those who are still using an older version of IOS can also avoid this malware by not allowing the installation of certificates unless it is from their company's IT department.

For IOS users, downloading apps only from the App Store can minimize the risk of malware. It does not mean that Android users are safer, though. Malware writers are invading Google Play by creating fake apps that mimic original apps, but with additional malware. Google has to monitor millions of apps and ensuring that apps do not have malware is not easy. There is a way to avoid potential malware, though. If an Android app asks for unnecessary permissions during installation, do not install it.

Fortunately, antivirus companies now have versions for both the IOS and Android platforms. Installing these apps will help users screen potential malware during installation, as well as remove malware that were accidentally installed.

Conclusion

Thank you again for purchasing this book!

I hope this book was able to help you understand malware threats to prevent them from spreading.

The next step is to check your computers for signs of malware and apply the lessons in this book to avoid infections in the future.

Finally, if you enjoyed this book, please take the time to share your thoughts and post a review on Amazon. It'd be greatly appreciated!

Thank you and good luck!

www.ingramcontent.com/pod-product-compliance
Lightning Source LLC
Chambersburg PA
CBHW070902070326
40690CB00009B/1958